W9-ABU-107

Date: 1/13/12

J 635.94 WEI
Weiss, Ellen,
From bulb to daffodil /

PALM BEACH COUNTY
LIBRARY SYSTEM
3650 SUMMIT BLVD.
WEST PALM BEACH, FL 33406

■ SCHOLASTIC
News
Nonfiction Readers

From Bulb to Daffodil

by Ellen Weiss

Children's Press®
A Division of Scholastic Inc.
New York Toronto London Auckland Sydney
Mexico City New Delhi Hong Kong
Danbury, Connecticut

These content vocabulary word builders are for grades 1–2.

Subject Consultant: Pati Vitt, PhD, Institute for Plant Conservation Biology,
Chicago Botanic Garden, Glencoe, Illinois

Reading Consultant: Cecilia Minden-Cupp, PhD, Early Literacy Consultant and Author,
Chapel Hill, North Carolina

Photographs © 2008: Alamy Images: 19, 21 top right (Gregory Davies), 1, 4 top, 17, 21 center right (Paul Lane, GardenWorld Images), cover right inset, 4 bottom left, 7, 20 right, 21 left (Chuck Pefley); Photo Researchers, NY: cover left inset, 2, 5 top right, 7 inset, 20 top left (Alan L. Detrick), 5 bottom left, 10, 16 (Adam Jones); Photolibrary: back cover, 4 bottom right, 13 (Chris Burrows), 11, 20 bottom (John Glover); ShutterStock, Inc.: 23 top right (Allyie Edwards), cover center inset, 5 top left, 15, 21 bottom (luminouslens), 23 bottom right (Artis Rams), 23 top left (Jenny Woodworth); Superstock, Inc./age fotostock: cover background; Visuals Unlimited: 5 bottom right, 9, 20 center left (Wally Eberhart), 23 bottom left (Jerome Wexler).

Book Design: Simonsays Design!
Book Production: The Design Lab

Library of Congress Cataloging-in-Publication Data
Weiss, Ellen, 1949–
From Bulb to Daffodil / by Ellen Weiss.
    p. cm.—(Scholastic news nonfiction readers)
Includes bibliographical references and index.
ISBN-13: 978-0-531-18534-6 (lib. bdg.) 978-0-531-18787-6 (pbk.)
ISBN-10: 0-531-18534-6 (lib. bdg.) 0-531-18787-X (pbk.)
1. Daffodils—Juvenile literature. 2. Bulbs—Juvenile literature. I. Title. II. Series.
SB413.D12W44 2007
635.9'3434—dc22   2007004767

No part of this publication may be reproduced in whole or in part, or stored in a retrieval system, or transmitted in any form or by any means, electronic, mechanical, photocopying, recording, or otherwise, without written permission of the publisher. For information regarding permission, write to Scholastic, 557 Broadway, New York, NY 10012.

©2008 Scholastic.
All rights reserved. Published in 2008 by Children's Press, an imprint of Scholastic Inc.
Published simultaneously in Canada. Printed in the United States of America. 44
SCHOLASTIC, CHILDREN'S PRESS, and associated logos are trademarks
and/or registered trademarks of Scholastic Inc.
1 2 3 4 5 6 7 8 9 10 R 17 16 15 14 13 12 11 10 09 08

CONTENTS

WORD HUNT

Look for these words as you read. They will be in **bold**.

blooms
(bloomz)

daffodils
(**daf**-fuh-dilz)

layers
(**lay**-urz)

4

buds
(buhdz)

bulbs
(buhlbs)

leaves
(leevz)

roots
(roots)

5

Growing Daffodils

Aren't these **daffodils** pretty?

Gardeners planted this field of flowers.

They did not plant seeds.

They planted **bulbs**. A bulb can grow into a new plant.

bulbs

We plant bulbs in the fall before winter begins.

Most bulbs need a cold winter before they grow.

In the soil, **roots** begin to grow from the bottom of the bulb.

roots

Roots help the growing plant get the water it needs.

A bulb is packed with all kinds of amazing things.

Inside each bulb is a tiny plant, ready to burst out.

There are tiny **leaves**, stems, and flower parts.

leaves

This daffodil is just starting to grow!

A bulb is also stuffed with food.

The food gives the tiny plant the energy it needs to grow.

The food is stored in **layers**.

If you cut a bulb in half, you can see the layers.

food

Can you see the layers of food inside this bulb?

When spring comes, daffodil bulbs grow **buds**.

Buds are small parts of plants that grow into leaves and flowers.

Soon the buds poke up out of the ground.

Sometimes the buds are called shoots.

Daffodils grow in the spring.

The daffodil plants keep growing.

You can see green leaves.

Soon, the flower buds are ready to open.

Look at the flowers!

They are called **blooms**.

flower bud

The center of a daffodil bloom is sometimes called the cup.

After a time, the flower turns brown and dies.

The green leaves keep making food for a few weeks.

The food is stored in the bulb.

The bulb will help a tiny new plant grow next spring!

This daffodil flower has died, but the green leaves are still busy making food for next spring.

DAFFODIL LIFE CYCLE

1 A bulb is planted.

2 Roots begin to grow.

3 Shoots appear above the ground.

6

The blooms die, but the bulb will grow again next year.

5

The daffodil blooms!

4

The plants grow and grow.

21

YOUR NEW WORDS

blooms (bloomz) flowers on plants

buds (buhdz) small shoots on plants that grow into leaves and flowers

bulbs (buhlbs) underground plant parts from which some plants, such as daffodils, grow

daffodils (**daf**-fuh-dilz) plants with long, narrow leaves and bell-shaped flowers

layers (**lay**-urz) several thicknesses of something, one on top of the other

leaves (leevz) the flat, usually green, parts of plants that make food for plants

roots (roots) the parts of plants that grow underground and absorb water from the soil

HERE ARE SOME OTHER PLANTS THAT GROW FROM BULBS

hyacinth
(**hye**-uh-sinth)

lily
(**lil**-ee)

onion
(**uhn**-yuhn)

tulip
(**too**-lip)

INDEX

FIND OUT MORE

Book:

Fowler, Allan. *It Could Still Be A Flower*. New York: Children's Press, 2001.

Website:

National Gardening Association's Kids Garden News: Bulbs!
www.kidsgardening.com/2005.kids.garden.news/sept/pg1.html#bg

MEET THE AUTHOR

Ellen Weiss has received many awards for her books for kids. She has a garden, where she is especially good at growing weeds.